DISCOVERING GOD'S PURPOSE FOR YOUR LIFE

DR. GREGORY CHILESHE

ISBN: 978-9982-70-640-7

Cover Design: Shadreck Mwaba

Supported: Richard Kamanga, Teddy Chushi and Omega Champions

First Editing/Layout: Kelvin C. Mwamba

Second Editing: Peter Whiteson Watema

Third and Final Editing: Professor Keller-USA

For details and orders:

+260763988703/+260950595611/ +260979011557
Email:doctorgregorypublications@gmail.com
:chileshegregory@gmail.com
Visit Web: drgregorychileshe.com

TABLE OF CONTENTS

Dedication

I wish to dedicate this book to my first-born daughter Natasha and also other unborn children to come, and grow and succeed with what it offers to generations to come especially to the children.

I also dedicate it to the one I love, also to the country of my origin and to the whole world; especially to you the reader so that you all can move in God's will or pattern for the rest of your lives and fulfill the reason why you came here on earth.

I also dedicate it to the following families: The Chisando and Mulenga families from my mother's side, the Chama and the Kang'ombe family from my father's side so that they also fulfill their lives in the exact plan and purpose of God.

Above all, I dedicate this book to the Holy Ghost, my ever Partner, Helper, Comforter,

Teacher, Lawyer, and Counselor etc. given to me by God to fulfill my divine ministry. To God my heavenly Father and the Lord Jesus Christ I say thank you so much. Finally, my calling goes to the world, World Moving Ministries. By your grace I promise to release more books to the world through your help my God. I urge all that after reading this book to be a born-again Christian by receiving Jesus Christ into your life as your Lord and Personal Savior. That is the first step-foundation to fulfilling the exact purpose of your life as you walk in the path of His word and roadmap set for your life. The manual for your life is in the hands of God who knows you better before you were formed in your mother's womb; before you were born to the earth.

Enjoy this book and let it correct you, instruct you, and rebuke you. May God Almighty bless you!

INTRODUCTION

The purpose of this book is to help you discover God's purpose for your life. To help you know the will of God for your life. To bring you in line with your calling or grace. To allow you to realize the existing anointing. To show you if you have missed "His Will" in whatever you are doing. To bring you back to your divine call and position God gave you especially. That is if you lost your position. However, it will enlighten the realities of the people you are with, whether they too have lost "His will" or "Calling" or "Grace".

It is therefore going to help you know who you are; your purpose for living and why you are here on earth. And why you are found in that position you are in today.

Do you have the right people within and surrounding your life? Discovering God's purpose for your life, will aid the end user with information on how to walk in the right plan

"God's Will". If you are in the right place or area where you are operating, then you do not need to worry yourself because this will act as a guide towards revitalizing the hidden abilities within your God given mandate to freely express your gifts and exude your life's mission.

In this life, you will realize that not only will you realign your potential, but also learn that your life is about "timing". And there's indeed no time to waste when it comes to knowledge that everything that has a beginning has an ending; you can't be in it forever. Now is the time to show that you can't be everything, but can be anything in this life. That you were called to a specific assignment, in a specific locality, family, country or continent, to a specific time zone, with a specific message and designation.

It is possible in life to not be intertwined as a general player. You were not called to do everything, but a specific thing. There are a lot of things to learn in this pursuit. You can also learn why certain revelations don't come to pass. Why some do come to pass, and which ones come to pass. They are there to teach the secret about God's speaking and how He comes to fulfill what He said and doesn't fulfill according to your timing or thinking or you helping Him. He stands by what He says and if God said something in your life, He will back it up to see it come to pass. Whether you or anybody likes it or not, whether they support it or not, whether you help God or not. He does not need your help anyway, He just needs your presence or your part if He tells you to, but He gets the glory in all He does.

Don't wreck or ruin your life. You can come back to the line of your calling and assignment God gave you at first.

Thank you and God bless you.

Chapter

-1-

INTRODUCTION TO GRACE

1Corinthians 2:1-5

"And I, brethren, when I came to you, came not with excellency of speech or of wisdom, declaring unto you the testimony of God. For I determined not to know any thing among you, save Jesus Christ, and him crucified. And I was with you in weakness, and in fear, and in much trembling. And my speech and my preaching was not with enticing words of man's wisdom, but in demonstration of the Spirit and of power: That your faith should not stand

in the wisdom of men, but in the power of God."(KJV)

Grace: Unmerited divine assistance given to humans for their regeneration or sanctification; a virtue coming from God; a state of sanctification enjoyed through divine assistance; a special favour; disposition to or an act or instance of kindness, courtesy, or clemency; a temporary exemption. **(Merriam Webster Dictionary)**

Grace is unmerited favor. Meaning you don't put in any effort or scoring any merit like distinction in order to qualify in something. In grace you don't need to qualify. God qualifies you. He works on behalf of you what you were supposed to do. In other words, it is the Lord's doing and it is marvelous.

Psalm 118:23-24

"This is the LORD's doing; It is marvellous in our eyes. This is the day which the LORD hath made; We will rejoice and be glad in it." (KJV)

Let us relook at what Paul said from the scripture quoted above: *"...when I came to you, came not with excellency of speech or of wisdom...I determined not to know any thing among you...I was with you in weakness, and in fear, and in much trembling...my speech and my preaching was not with enticing words of man's wisdom, but in demonstration of the Spirit and of power: THAT YOUR FAITH SHOULD NOT STAND IN THE WISDOM OF MEN, but in the power of God."* (KJV)

That was grace. Paul was talking about grace. He was showing them that it was not about the wisdom of men, but the power of God when testifying to them how he started. He didn't go to them with the wisdom of men. Paul was very educated, but he didn't use his levels of education to convince them about Christ. He went in the demonstration of the Spirit and power.

In this book, I am first introducing you to the word 'grace' for a purpose. So that understanding of the word 'grace' opens you up to know what is happening in your life if you missed your grace or not. This is what this book is all about. It is to cause you to discover your grace. If you missed it somewhere to know what has happened or what you have been doing if it was right or wrong.

If you are truly born again, you will know the will of God in your life through conscience.

You will know through the inward witness, still small voice, and authoritative voice of God or divine vision. Depend on grace not the wisdom of men.

I wrote this book "DISCOVERING GOD'S PURPOSE FOR YOUR LIFE" specifically to make you know who you are. To help you know what to do when you are doubting your calling especially when you believe that you have listened to God, but you are not sure if He spoke to you or not. A good example is the apostle, Paul.

To deal with any doubt about his call and purpose on earth, Paul always depended on a vision from God revealed to him on his way to Damascus. That was the grace he found. He may have doubted other things about his calling, but not this encounter with Jesus Christ on his way to Damascus. He was always strengthened by this vision every time he remembered it. The vision was real that is why he always testified about it.

In this same vision Paul was warned by Jesus Christ that it was Him he was fighting, and not necessarily His people, the believers, who he was joyfully attacking.

It was stated that it was hard for him to **"...kick against the pricks..."** Pricks are known to be sharp-pointed instruments in front such as a needle or a sharp-pointed knife. Jesus was referring to Himself as the one being fought against. Destiny or pre-destiny set by God cannot be destroyed. Kicking in front of pricks is injuring you. You will be hurting yourself. You cannot win that war. It is like destroying yourself. If you succeed infighting God's servant, it may be that God has just permitted it that way by removing His immunity (protection) from His own for the purpose of growing His own person from faith to faith. Otherwise, that is a dangerous move.

Another good example is Job, the man of God. God boasted about Job and permitted the Devil to try him. Other than that, if God has not allowed it, you may be a dead man or woman who is doing that to His anointed and chosen one of God because God's coverage on a person is immunity given. Whoever assumes to touch, without His permission, Goodwill respond.

God has always responded to such attacks on His people before and several examples in the Bible are there such as attacking Moses on his decision to marry, a king trying to sleep with Abraham's wife etc.

You can't curse whom God has not cursed. You can reverse a curse, but you can't reverse a blessing. Take an example of Barak son of Zippor, King of the Moabites and Balaam son of Beor who failed to curse a blessed nation. Numbers 22:1-41, mind especially 'verse 12', then proceed to chapter 23:1-30, also mind especially 'verses 8 and 23', then proceed to chapter 24:1 going forward. The end of the attacker will be worse than what he did to God's own. He says, *"touch not the anointed ones and do my prophets no harm."*

It is God who will punish or discipline His own if there is error, not any Jim and Jack.

Acts 9:1-8

"And Saul, yet breathing out threatening and slaughter against the disciples of the Lord, went unto the high priest, And desired of him letters to Damascus to the synagogues, that if he found any of this way, whether they were men or women, he might bring them bound unto Jerusalem.

And as he journeyed, he came near Damascus: and suddenly there shined round about him a light from heaven: And he fell to the earth, and heard a voice saying unto him, Saul, Saul, why persecutest thou me? And he said, Who art thou, Lord?

And the Lord said, I am Jesus whom thou persecutest: *it is* hard for thee to kick against the pricks. And he trembling and astonished said, Lord, what wilt thou have me to do? And the Lord *said* unto him, Arise, and go into the city, and it shall be told thee what thou must do. And the men which journeyed with him stood speechless, hearing a voice, but seeing no man. And Saul arose from the earth; and when his eyes were opened, he saw no man: but they led him by the hand, and brought *him* into Damascus." (KJV)

A Journey of "discovering God's purpose for your life" can make you encounter a lot of things in life. You may not know the reason why you are here on earth. You may go through ups and downs. This can be worse if you are so ignorant about the word of God and the leading of the Spirit. This can also depend on the careless decisions you make in life. If you choose a wrong path in knowing who you are or a wrong office of your calling, it may land your life into difficult situations. Certain paths are outside the will of God. You may not notice fast. If you make a wrong decision on the anointing to flow in, life can be terrible for you. Such are the challenges that can cause you to suffer to the realization point until you are back in line with the will of God.

Some bad decisions can cause you to cry before God. Meditate in His word until He reveals to you where you missed it, if you did.

Some situations may just be a test to perfect you. God can turn your situation into a blessing like it happened to Job in the Bible.

This book will now make you reposition yourself into your God given position if you lost it. It is a book to correct you and to bring your life back on the correct path before you leave this earth.

POSITION OF YOUR GRACE

There are certain things God can allow you to do, but He leads your heart not to stay longer in it because you are just allowed as a free moral agent to make your independent decisions. A prodigal son story reveals a permissive will of God. God may allow you to do something under His permissive will and lead you back to your grace or assignment you were born for as the perfect will of God. Like a prodigal son story, if you are lost in His will, you should also get back to Him for a perfect will of God to flow in and He will receive you as he did to the lost son and prepared ceremonious meal, a banquet. That is what He wants.

There are certain situations God Himself allows, but just briefly because they are not your exact area of call. God has worked with me a lot in what I call **interventions**. Sometimes I stayed longer in some of them, wasting time because liked them anyway, but they were not directly connected to the call of God or grace given to me. It meant that I was just called upon to intervene. Some of these interventions have been exciting. You would even think you have arrived when you are flowing in them, when they were not your full grace, but something like. You may not understand this, but only when you find yourself flow in the same. I realized in the scripture Paul understood this.

Paul in the Scripture said, "**I can do all things through Christ who strengthens me.**" And he meant **all things,** not just some things or one thing. That should not make you leave your calling or anointing because you can do all things. You must always remember that you are not a general player on earth even if you can be. You were called to do a specific thing. You are specific. You are here on earth specifically. Paul was called to Gentiles not to the Jews, but sometimes under permissive will he would preach to Jews. He rebuked Peter before.

Galatians 2:11-13

"But when Peter came to Antioch, I had to oppose him to his face, for what he did was very wrong. When he first arrived, he ate with the Gentile believers, who were not circumcised. But afterward, when

some friends of James came, Peter wouldn't eat with the Gentiles anymore. He was afraid of criticism from these people who insisted on the necessity of circumcision. As a result, other Jewish believers followed Peter's hypocrisy, and even Barnabas was led astray by their hypocrisy." (NLT)

Even though the author of the book of Hebrews is not mentioned by name, it is believed that Paul was the Author and if it was Paul, then he was speaking to the Jews. Jews are Hebrews. That may sound like permissive will when he crossed the lines to rebuke Peter for siding with the Jews.

23

Chapter

-2-

MINDING TIME ON YOUR LIFE

Psalms 90:10

"The days of our years are threescore years and ten; and if by reason of strength they be fourscore years, yet is their strength labour and sorrow; for it is soon cut off, and we fly away." (KJV)

Minding time for your life is very, very important.

Ephesians 5:15-17

"then that ye walk circumspectly, not as fools, but as wise, Redeeming the time, because the days are evil. Wherefore be ye not unwise, but understanding what the will of the Lord is" (KJV)

To be mindful of time in life is very important. If you don't mind, you may find yourself gone from the earth at a time you were not ready or prepared to finish the assignment God brought you for here on earth. You need to be time conscious. You should always mind. Work with estimates, conscious and redeeming time. Ask yourself, "from this point, before that point comes, what is it that I should do or what is it that should be done? And what is it I am doing in line with God's call on my life? Is it in line with the purpose I was born for?"

Three score and ten years. The Bible is talking about three score being 60 years and four score is 80 years. You and I may go up to

70 years in energy for maximum performance and if we have enough strength we may reach even up to 80 years, but life is soon cut off and we fly away. Some will even die before 70 years and in lower ages below 70 years; they will be dead, and many have died. This was the reality for those who murmured against God and refused to enter the Promised Land. In other words, there is no time to waste here on earth on the assignment God has given you if you have discovered it. If you have not, invest everything in trying to know who you are. Associate with the right people greater than you who have made it in life to help you know who you are. And, you do not have to be limited to 70-80 years when God has already fixed man's time on earth as 120 years (Genesis 6:3).

(Proverbs 28:5)

"Evil men understand not judgment: but they that seek the LORD understand all things."

28

Chapter

-3-

STAY IN LINE WITH YOUR PURPOSE

Romans 9:19-22

"Thou wilt say then unto me, why doth he yet find fault? For who hath resisted his will? Nay but, O man, who art thou that repliest against God? Shall the thing formed say to him that formed it, Why hast thou made me thus? Hath not the potter power over the clay, of the same lump to make one vessel unto honour, and another unto dishonour? What if God, willing to shew his wrath, and to make his power known, endured with much

*longsuffering the vessels of wrath fitted
to destruction.”* (KJV)

Proverbs 20:18

*“Every purpose is established by counsel:
and with good advice make war.”* (KJV)

Joel 2:4, 7-8

*“The appearance of them is as the
appearance of horses; and as horsemen, so
shall they run. They shall run like mighty
men; they shall climb the wall like men of
war; and they shall march every one on
his ways, and they shall not break their
ranks: Neither shall one thrust another;
they shall walk every one in his path: and
when they fall upon the sword, they shall
not be wounded.”* (KJV)

You could be going in line with the vision, but that could contrast the meaning of not going in line with the purpose of your life. You may fulfill a vision, but it is not in line with your life or in line with your purpose on earth. Your purpose goes in line with your calling. Your calling goes in line with your purpose. Make sure you are sensitive with your calling, sensitive with your purpose, the purpose for your life.

Anything that disturbs your calling or your purpose in life, don't stay in it. If you are in it, don't stay for a long time. Find ways and means to be back on track. Don't be excited with what it offers. Even if you are enjoying, you may be deceived. It may be temporal. You must discern the spirit and act accordingly.

You may experience very bad things at a later stage. You may experience calamities or torture. Things may begin to break down.

Things may begin to tumble and make you tremble. They may begin to fall out and apart and punish you and everything you have may get destroyed, including your marriage, family, business, and relationship with good friends.

Be circumspect, you may end up pulling many people into trouble just like Jonah. Jonah thought he would escape. He thought he would run away from the assignment which was divine and appointed for him by God in line with his destiny. But Jonah's mission failed because the assignment he denied was in line with his purpose. It was in line with his call. Because of that, he survived. Without that he would not have survived in the waters and from the mouth of the fish. God is always gracious with the disobedient. He gave Jonah grace in the belly of the fish, the place of suffering and huge torture. That is what the belly of the fish represented. It was a death sentence awaiting Jonah's confession of repentance and regret for a decision outside of God's program. Remember that it is only you He wants to use and bring you this purpose here on earth. In such times God acts in righteous judgment to correct the errant servant. He is not a man that He should lie by breaking His promises or words He spoke.

Even Jesus Christ in His time on earth made sure He was in line with His call and purpose.

Matthew 16:21-23

"from that time forth began Jesus to shew unto his disciples, how that he must go unto Jerusalem, and suffer many things of the elders and chief priests and scribes, and be killed, and be raised again the third day. Then Peter took him, and began to rebuke him, saying, be it far from thee, Lord: this shall not be unto thee. But he turned, and said unto Peter, Get thee behind me, Satan: thou art an

offence unto me: for thou savourest not the things that be of God, but those that be of men. ” (KJV)

GIFTS IN LINE WITH YOUR CALLING

Romans 12:3

“For I say, through the grace given unto me, to every man that is among you, not to think of himself more highly than he ought to think; but to think soberly, according as God hath dealt to every man the measure of faith. ” (KJV)

Romans 12:6-8

“Having then gifts differing according to the grace that is given to us, whether prophecy, let us prophesy according to the proportion of faith; Or ministry, let us wait on our ministering: or he that teacheth, on teaching; Or he that

exhorteth, on exhortation: he that giveth, let him do it with simplicity; he that ruleth, with diligence; he that sheet mercy, with cheerfulness." (KJV)

God makes sure everyone born is equipped with the full kit to succeed in his or her life. You are born fully equipped. All the gifts in you are meant to fulfill your purpose; the reason why you are here; the reason why you are born. Find your gifts; know your gifts. They are like minerals. Minerals are mined because they are hidden. Find a gift that is according to God's plan.

If you mine gifts easily without going some process, it is just because God is showing you that there's a potent core purpose deep within your life. And truth be told, you can't just pick things easily on the surface as you go through life today. It may just mean the place is a rich area. So, if you just pick one mineral piece and got satisfied with it to get you rich, but you may end up missing the whole thing under the ground. Instead you extend to dig deep - go deeper. This should be the same way to know the riches God has embedded in you and on you. What you are good at is called talent. There are spiritual gifts and natural gifts. Spiritual gifts are first spiritually discerned. They cannot be seen openly until they are manifested. Natural gifts manifesto the outside, seen by the physical world. Spiritual gifts are invisible until you make them visible to people through God who is invisible.

I Corinthians 12:1, 4-11

"Now concerning spiritual gifts, brethren, I would not have you ignorant. Now there are diversities of gifts, but the same Spirit. And there are differences of administrations, but the same Lord. And there are diversities of operations, but it is the same God which

worketh all in all. But the manifestation of the Spirit is given to every man to profit withal."

"For to one is given by the Spirit the word of wisdom; to another the word of knowledge by the same Spirit; To another faith by the same Spirit; to another the gifts of healing by the same Spirit; To another the working of miracles; to another prophecy; to another discerning of spirits; to another divers kinds of tongues; to another the interpretation of tongues: But all these worketh that one and the selfsame Spirit, dividing to every man severally as he will." (KJV)

Find your life gifts in full. Natural gifts which don't manifest, but show as they are, naturally seen or spiritual gifts which manifest from the spiritual. E.g. Physical gifts such as Politics are through the mouth not the legs or hands.

Football is on the legs and not the mouth that is why that talent is called 'Foot-ball'. You don't even need prayer for it to manifest. You just need to practice to become perfect, but you can't practice spiritual gifts. They are not natural to be rehearsed or perfected. Natural gifts are what are called talents. We should not expect them to manifest. They are directly seen on the body and mostly, from what I have discovered, are prominently found on three parts of the body and that is on the mouth, on the hands-arms and then on the legs. They come through the mouth, the hands-arms and the legs. Check these talents on those three parts, they are many to count. Speech or speaking is through the mouth and not the legs. Repairing is through the hands, boxing is on the hands, computers touched by the hands though involved the brain and so on.

You may have many gifts in you, but make sure the prominent ones are followed and developed. Those which are prominent are known as major gifts; those which are not are known as minor gifts. But there are also other major gifts different from those and these are called the fivefold ministry gifts or graces, these are spiritual offices. The office of an Apostle, office of an Evangelist, office of a Prophet, office of a Pastor and a Teacher.

Ephesians 4:7-12

"But unto every one of us is given grace according to the measure of the gift of Christ. Wherefore he saith, when he ascended up on high, he led captivity captive, and gave gifts unto men. (Now that he ascended, what is it but that he also descended first into the lower parts of the earth? He that descended is the same also that ascended up far above all heavens, that he might fill all things.) And he gave some apostles; and some, prophets; and some, evangelists;

and some, pastors and teachers; for the perfecting of the saints, for the work of the ministry, for the edifying of the body of Christ." (KJV)

41

Chapter

-4-

ANOINTING DOES NOT DIE

Romans 11:29

"For the gifts and calling of God are without repentance" (KJV)

II Kings 13:21

And it came to pass, as they were burying a man, that, behold, they spied a band of men; and they cast the man into the sepulchre of Elisha: and when the man was let down, and touched the bones of Elisha, he revived, and stood up on his feet. (KJV)

The anointing does not die. It can go with you to the grave if there is no one to take it up and can still work in the grave like it woke up someone who fell on the bones of a man of God, Elisha.

The anointing is like a relay button in a relay race or sport. The anointing is like a number in a football match.

1. THE ANOINTING AS A RELAY BUTTON

The anointing itself handled on earth by God, if this is His particular duty or purpose specifically, does not die. That kind of button does not die. It just moves from one person to another.

The anointing which was upon Abraham was relayed upon Isaac. The anointing which was on Isaac was relayed upon Jacob who became known as Israel which we know today as a country. So, this same anointing of a person is on a nation now. Israel has this anointing, dressed by it; covered by it; defended by it.

This same anointing prospered Jacob suddenly and has done the same to Israel.

Anointing is like a seed. A seed will maintain the name of the plant and the fruit. For as long as the seed does not get destroyed, the fruit will continue coming out as it is called and known. That is the anointing, it is transferable. One's anointing is the same, it just repeats itself.

2. THE ANOINTING LIKE A NUMBER IN FOOTBALL OR ANY OTHER GAME THAT USES NUMBERS

There are many examples. However, numbers are not the ones substituted in football, for example, it is a player. A player leaves the number vacant, and a replacement is brought in to replace the one substituted and the one who enters on that number is expected to play better than the one who was there. Has the number died or changed? The answer is "No" instead it is a person changed. Somebody has taken the same number to play the same number.

Know your number, know your anointing. Know who is playing your number or using your anointing. And by this, I mean a similar anointing. John the Baptist did flow in the spirit and power of Elijah. Elisha did flow in the spirit and power of Elijah. The coach, in this case, is God. He is the one who knows who can be substituted. He is the one who knows who is playing well or just walking with the number without producing the results of the purpose of that number.

So the anointing is like a relay button or a number in football or sports. There is no death to the number or the relay button until the world ends. Examples have been why God is called the God of Abraham, Isaac and Jacob. We still have Jacob in the name of Israel. The Jews are connected to this anointing-blessing. Everyone who becomes born again becomes a

Jew spiritually by engraftment and joins in this anointing line called the Abrahamic covenant of health, prosperity, enlargement anointing, etc.

Elijah relayed the button to Elisha. Elijah was substituted from the number (anointing) he was playing and replaced by Elisha who got double the anointing because the task ahead was amplified. Moses was replaced by Joshua. Saul was replaced by David. David was replaced by Solomon. There are many examples that we can refer to. Alas, the anointing keeps going from one generation to another.

John the Baptist rose in the spirit and power of Elijah and it was stated. He rose in the anointing of Elijah meaning he started doing everything like Elijah not because he wanted, but because of the type of anointing or number he put on.

The anointing remains to be succeeded; it doesn't die. Not everyone can be a doctor, a teacher, a soldier, a president, a nurse, a policeman, a footballer, a musician etc. Check your gifts. Are they spiritual or natural? Check what you like most. Choose who you like most. It may be in line with your anointing and anointing does not lie and same with God's purpose or vision, it doesn't die or lie.

FIND YOUR GRACE

Act 10:38

"How God anointed Jesus of Nazareth with the Holy Ghost and with power: who went about doing good, and healing all that were oppressed of the devil; for God was with him." (KJV)

You can't be a jack-of-all-trades. Thus, it is extremely important first of all to be anointed. Many people are anointed in various pursuits and ways. Many are such anointed, yet they perhaps don't know or realize so. You are called specifically, not generally.

Do you know the reason why you were born in a specific family, in a specific area or place with a specific purpose? That is something you and I both need to take into consideration today. Born in a specific Province or City or State; in a specific Country; in a specific Continent; with a specific complexion; to a specific people representing them fully in a time such as now. Whether you are currently in the USA or in the UK, for as long as you were not born there or you were born there, as we can put it though not truly so, you are a representative of your family to that country and continent of origin. Bear the candle wherever you are, because God will judge you because He never made a mistake for you to be born in a specific place.

To copy is not bad, but to change what you are is a violation of God's restraining orders and purpose. It is definitely for a reason and God did not make a mistake about your birth right and that for you to correct Him; as to why you are who you are and where you are today, it is like saying why did you create me in your likeness? It is a violation of God's wisdom or thinking capacity.

What does God expect of you? Of course, [1] you never chose to be what He made you, and [2] there is no reason for bargaining or begging. You are what you are, there is no mistake at all which God made, just love yourself and learn from other people's achievements and make it. God brought you here on earth and to the area where you are as a change maker to that horizon and designation. If you haven't arrived at your glorified locale of grace, or place of operation with the right people, He still will redirect your existence towards your heart's desire and purpose.

Keep standing on His word in prayer. In other words, you are still moving, like Abraham was told to go to a place he did not know, realigning him according to his purpose to the place of his purpose to fulfill the assignments for the reason why he was born. Everybody has a reason he or she was born for; everyone has a purpose. You were born with a purpose, and you can't and should not live without. Everything here on earth has a purpose. Stones have a purpose, rivers have a purpose, animals have a purpose, rains have a purpose, a machine made by man has a purpose, a phone has a purpose, a vehicle has a purpose, a spoon has a purpose etc.

How can you be born without a purpose? How can you be the only moving thing without a purpose like a headless chicken which doesn't know or see where it is going? And can there be a life in such a thing moving headless? For how long can that be? Couldn't we have seen one? But that would amount to magic or witchcraft or Satanism if we did see one moving with no head. You cannot be allowed to exist on earth like that. There are no such creatures on earth, maybe in the darkness as fiction. It is against God's nature or creation. It is a breaking of the earthly protocol of living and against God's orders of creation.

Don't move without God's plan for your life. You are under restraining orders like Adam and Eve was according to the sphere of operation. God sets rules, limits, boundaries, and distance according to His plan for your life. Be with God, move with God the owner of your life. Lean not unto your own understanding.

God has called you to a specific assignment, to a specific area and to a specific people. You can't be everything to everyone. Not everyone will be preached to by you. Not everyone will be reached by you. Not everyone will be your fan. Not everyone will hear you or love you or like you and you cannot please everybody. God did not call you to do that, and it will never happen no matter how good or smart you are, or else you lose your own soul as the Bible puts in trying to please everyone or win the world. It is not attainable. That goal cannot be achieved.

God called you to a specific people, with a specific message. Discern everything and move according to His will, according to His word and Spirit.

Every minister or leader or person is limited. You have to find your anointing or your grace boundaries; what you are anointed in or anointed for or what you are graced in. You cannot preach or teach everything or preach like others do but find your anointing or your grace. Find your area of operation or area of teaching or preaching and you will become great as a minister of God. You will become great as a called person or as an individual here on earth. Your life is too short according to God's way of seeing things and creation.

The maximum is 120 years, but 70-80 is the period you may perform lastly there after you may have no power to. This is something worthy of consideration to the point of having it in your head and in your heart. Do not allow yourself to be limited by 70-80 years. A day to God can be a thousand and a thousand to God can be a day. You are not here for a joke. You are here for a reason and that reason is a purpose and if that reason is the purpose why you are here, that is the anointing you carry. It is in line with the purpose. They cannot be separate. They are together and nobody can destroy that for as long as it was sanctioned by God Himself. So, know the reason you are here. Know the reason; know the purpose which is the reason why; know your anointing; know your grace; know your call; know your gifts.

The key point to know is to continue to flow in preaching (Word) and to continue to pray for people by faith (Spirit-action). God honors His word. Speak His word if you want Him to move. If you want a miracle from Him. He doesn't operate outside His word. You can't move Him by anything. You can't move Him by any standard other than what He has set for Himself. He is supreme, above everything and you can't lower Him to your level or any level of standard you think against what He is.

Mark 16:15-20

"And he said unto them, Go ye into all the world, and preach the gospel to every creature. He that believeth and is baptized shall be saved; but he that believeth not shall be damned. And

these signs shall follow them that believe; In my name shall they cast out devils; they shall speak with new tongues; They shall take up serpents; and if they drink any deadly thing, it shall not hurt them; they shall lay hands on the sick, and they shall recover. So then after the Lord had spoken unto them, he was received up into heaven, and sat on the right hand of God. And they went forth, and preached everywhere, the Lord working with them, and confirming the word with signs following. Amen." (KJV)

There is no mistake to your line. Your line or grace or call or gift will always show if you are in service-working. It will always prove and bring you before great men. Your line of flow will always be approved and blessed by God. God will always approve and bless His will.

Outside His plan or will, there is limited grace (little grace). Meaning each one is limited in his or her call or grace. If you go beyond that, it is a violation of grace or God's restraining orders unless under permissive will God permits you, but even if; it is, but temporary. He expects you to quickly get back to your line because if you go beyond your grace, there is no coverage beyond it. You have to provide coverage for yourself. What you are not called in, there is limited grace because it is not your office. But it belongs to another person's office or place, and they will feel very good and feel arrived, but you will not because it is not in you.

You will be uncomfortable, and you will have no peace. There will be a lot of mistakes and troubles. With you not being in your field, there will be no peace and provision. Where you think there is no peace and provision for, there is peace and provision for another person anointed for it and that person is enjoying to the maximum while you are going down. You will be finished to the last if you don't sense fast or seek proper advice or guidance from the right people.

You will never succeed in the wrong place or grace, no matter who helps you, no matter the investment you can make. It is just a waste of time and resources and years and life. Look for Capernaum; go to Capernaum (your area or grace where you are accepted, where your message is accepted). That was what Jesus did when there was little faith, He never hesitated.

So why should you even waste time? He left where they received Him not and where things were not happening. But we are busy doing one and the same thing. Doing the same thing which does not produce results and it qualifies to or graduates into madness as the English saying goes. Trying to obtain results from the same thing that is not giving you expected results. Think fast, change the formula, change the strategy, change the people, and change the place. But don't change what you are. It will be a violation and God will never honor the work because it springs from disobedience.

Don't even think there is a Devil there? How many times have you dealt with powers of darkness? And there are many people hunting you like house flies looking for dry fish. What God starts; He protects. What God starts; He defends. So why are you busy holding it when you are not responsible for it. There are things in the Bible Which God has told us clearly, He will take care, defend, and protect. Find them, not what is initiated by you. You will blunt yourself handling what is not your size. If He wanted you in, He would have told you. Check many examples God has in the Bible.

What a man can do, God will not come in no matter how much prayer and fasting you can do. What is within your capacity, God will not do it, do it yourself? If you have both hands to eat and all is okay, can you say God please feed me? That is tempting God. Just think! He is restrained in certain things He has done for a human being or given to a human being and other creatures. Make sure the next place you go to there is enough grace to survive by the Spirit of God and to know His will is there. The Holy Ghost will just flow willingly because it is in line with God. Jesus found His grace in Capernaum where there was provision of everything and re-launched His ministry from there.

Always being with 50 people or 100 people should not excite you unless your anointing is limited to that or just a local area anointing or a province or just a national anointing. As we call ourselves as national prophets or preachers because we are used by God and called to just speak to our country. That is national anointing, but there is also international anointing, which one are you in? Jeremiah was ordained Prophet unto the nations, not a nation. And we like speaking like that. Read the book of Jeremiah 1:5 and Acts 17:26, you will discover that not everyone was internationally anointed though the gospel is international, and it can go to any place on earth; to any human being, race, or color, but you may not reach the whole world as an individual.

Chapter

- 5 -

FIND YOUR PURPOSE

Jeremiah 1:5

"Before I formed thee in the belly I knew thee; and before thou camest forth out of the womb I sanctified thee, and I ordained thee a prophet unto the nations"

Act 17:26

And hath made...one blood all nations of men...to dwell on all the face of the earth, and hath determined the times before appointed..."

Define the word purpose in the first place:

PURPOSE: that which a person sets before himself as an object to be reached or accomplished; the end or aim to which the view is directed in any plan, measure, or exertion; view; aim; design; intention; plan.

Another definition: proposal to another, **discourse**.

So in this case you are not the one who designed or the one setting or designing this plan of living, God designed it before you were born. God designed your life; God measured your life, set it before you as an object or proposal to be reached or accomplished.

Now the question is, what is that purpose in your life, what is that proposal God has put to you, do you understand it? That is a huge task to ask God all the time to unveil it as the manufacturer of your life; the designer of it.

God is the purposer of your life for lack of better terms; one who forms a purpose; one who intends.

The word **discourse** is a conversation, a talk either written or unwritten. God had already done the talking or conversation about your life before it existed, written or unwritten. ***"In thy book all my members were written, which in continuance were fashioned, when as yet there was none of them."***

Psalm 139:5, 13

Thou **hast beset me behind and before, and laid thine hand upon me. For thou hast possessed my reins: thou hast covered me in my mother's womb**

Being covered physically and spiritually is also being anointed. The anointing is for cover; to hide you. It is immunity. It is the power to achieve God's purpose or plan over your life. You were actually anointed in your mother's womb. Covered by the inside membrane. The amniotic fluid covers the developing embryo or the baby from possible harm until it grows and faces the earth. That cover continues even after you are born until you achieve your life purpose unless you live outside His will, purpose or anointing which is what this book is addressing. Walking in disobedience to God allows Satan to take advantage and cause death at an early stage.

Psalm 139:14-18

I will praise thee; for I am fearfully and wonderfully made: marvelous are thy works; and that my soul knoweth right well. My substance was not hid from thee, when I was made in secret, and curiously wrought in the lowest parts of the earth. Thine eyes did see my substance, yet being unperfect; and in thy book all my members were written, which in continuance were fashioned, when as yet there was none of them. How precious also are thy thoughts unto me, O God! how great is the sum of them! If I should count them, they are more in number than the sand: when I awake, I am still with thee

Understanding it deeper; your purpose-life design must go with your plan. God's purpose in your life goes with God's plan over your life. This is what makes you prosper. If you miss His purpose and His plan, you miss His blessings or grace and all operations are outside His coverage.

The enemy will strike not because God did not see, but because you decided to be like a chick that leaves its mother's wings. Even when the mother keeps communicating to it and keeps bringing it under its wings together with the rest. Psalm 91:1, 4. But obedience is better than sacrifice. It is better to listen to God and not take advantage because He has given you free will to decide. The question to be asked and answered is, what is your purpose? Other people's individual purposes or individual plans are not supposed to be followed without sacrificial consideration. They are not your plans otherwise if not in line you will just be promoting another person and not yourself or your own individual purpose.

This is why you don't need to stay longer in what is not in line with your call no matter how sweet it may become to you such that it makes you forget and become enslaved. In such, to survive and push it in line with your gift, let it benefit your interests or call or grace first otherwise don't even venture in it or explore unless you have capacity to come out easily.

General purpose in a church is good and acceptable, but in this book we are talking about individual purpose.

Let that individual plan or purpose support your grace. If it doesn't then you are just fulfilling another man's grace who will receive a full reward from heaven without even considering your help. God didn't call you to help unless you were in that ministry called help ministry. Whether you are under someone or not it must be in line with your individual purpose. Whichever call or ordination you are in, founder or not; He called you to fulfill your individual purpose.

Whatever you do is not to support or help God; God counts it as fulfillment of what He put in you. Doing the work of God is not helping anybody, but you. It is to the glory of God and it counts for judgment and reward to an individual. God will reward us individually. Just find your position or place of purpose. Why was John called by the title 'Baptist' if it was not his purpose for being here on earth? That is why he was called John the Baptist because that was the purpose.

John the Baptist was not called to help Jesus Christ, but He was called to his purpose. He came on earth to do his part and that was to pave the way for Jesus. He came to baptize people and baptized Jesus. He came to make His path straight. John was to do his job and finish it and leave the earth. He did not come to argue with the king. That would be beyond his grace. For as long as your grace has finished the work, there is no grace beyond that point. And there was no grace beyond the point of everything John the Baptist finished to do as his purpose on earth. It was not a dignified death according to me though it may be a welcome passage to heaven by dying the way he died. We will put it in qualification of suffering for God and the truth.

Jesus was there and heard about the death of John who had the anointing of Elijah. Elijah did not test death, but John did. The death of John appeared to have pained Jesus. Jesus went to the mountain to make strong prayers to the point that He remained behind while others (His disciples) departed. I am sure His disciples in a boat were thinking they needed to see their families. They could not imitate Jesus by staying away from home to be in the mountains. That was the impact of the death of John the Baptist on Jesus Christ such that He decided to show that He was God in full control regardless of the human body He was in. Though He was in the body of a human being on earth He walked on water like it was walking on a tarred road. This shocked all His disciples who had taken the boat. He found them in the midst of the waves of the sea; walking on water like there was no wave. Peter wanted to prove if it was truly Jesus walking on the water. Jesus invited him. Peter tried to walk on water, but realized he was but human, lost faith in Jesus and began to sink into the water at the sight of the mighty waves.

I can imagine the words of Thomas and Philip causing the faith of the other people to fade. Probably they were the ones that discouraged Peter from going spiritual. Maybe he was reminded that he was but human in the body. Maybe they realized that Peter would drown and die even when he was before the face of the resurrection, Jesus Himself. But even if it did happen that he died he would be resurrected by Jesus Christ Himself.

No matter how sweet the grace you are in is. If the inward premonition tells you it is not the will of God to be in it then it was not meant for you, but for another. For as long as God does not bless you or increase you in it and does not give you peace, He will bless or increase the person it was meant for and give peace for it. You will have no peace in what is not the will of God for you. If there is no peace in what you are doing, it is not the will of God. God is not a fool to bless what He has not initiated. God's will back His own words and plans. If it is not the plan of God, it will be in your power to fulfill. To succeed by the will of God you have to divorce your plan and stick to His plan. And peace and grace would flow. You just have to be married to His plan to experience grace. There are no two ways about it. Otherwise, if you work in your own plan, you will fulfill your own plan and you will definitely fulfill it with labor-merit not with grace which does not require any merit or effort.

"Except the Lord build the house, they labor in vain that build it..."(Psalm 127:1).

Be cautious, you can have the right plan with the wrong purpose-design or pattern. You can have the right purpose-design or pattern, but with the wrong plan. The Bible says *"lean not on thine own understanding..."* The Bible guides that in all your ways acknowledge Him. That is what it means to walk in His plan or His purpose for your life. While you plan, you acknowledge Him to counter check you. It means to counter check if your plan is in line with His plan for your life. Without that, you are walking alone and not with God. A man of God is God's man. You can't be God's man if you don't walk and talk with Him. It means you walk alone. It means you are alone in ministry. And if you are always alone spiritually and not with God Almighty the creator of the universe, why should you be called a man of God? It is a mockery, Galatians 6:3-9. Always consult God. Prayer is consulting God. Always praying is always consulting, but it matters the kind of prayer. Not every prayer is a good prayer. Not every prayer is answerable prayer and not every prayer impresses God. Pray in line with His word in the Bible. You have to please Him at all times. Enough walked with God because He pleased God.

The prayer of faith in line with the will and plan of God is what brings answers. Faith without action is dead. It has no positive results. The prayer of faith in His will impresses Him. Without faith, and faith in His will, it is impossible to please Him. Praying in His will is praying according to His word. Pray correct prayers for God's anointing and grace to increase and to flow. Correct word-based prayers in the will of God can help you get back to your calling or grace or position you lost. Don't miss the will of God in your life.

You need to know your individual plan of God. Know your individual purpose of God for the salvation of many people.

"Before I formed thee in the belly I knew thee and before thou camest out of the womb I ordained thee a prophet unto the nations."(Jeremiah 1:5).

The **purpose** or reason or vision was to be a **prophet unto the nations**. The **calling** was to be **ordained as a prophet** unto the nations.

The **plan** was to **sanctify** him in order to change the nations or to make the nations hear His word of prophecy, not as any other calling, but as a prophet. You can't change a person if you are not changed first. Otherwise, you are effecting no change, but making a person worse than what you are. Example of this is when Jesus called the *"Pharisees whitewashed tombs"* due to hypocrisy, (Matthew 23:27).

To **sanctify is to separate**, not to be found with ordinary people. For Jeremiah, grace was in the ministry or office of a prophet, not any other ministry admired. That time in the Old Testament they were anointing three people which were a King, Prophet, and Priest. He was ordained or anointed as Prophet, but not like David. David was known to come to rule as both King and Prophet.

The grace of Prophet Jeremiah was to the nations and not to a nation. In other words, he was not a national prophet, but an international prophet. He had International grace not national grace, *"...unto the nations."*

Don't make your own plan and ask God to bless intuit will be your own plan, and not His plan. God can bless it or allow it, but He will not put the full approval and blessing to it if it is not initiated by Him. It will be what is known as permissive will and not perfect will of God. Permissive will in the sense that you are forcing God to hear you and do what you want. It will not be His plan and He will not protect it. You have to find ways and means to defend it and protect it yourself. What God has not started is not under His hands, but under your hands, you who started it. He can only help until you see and know that He is not in it.

"But when it pleased God, who separated me from my mother's womb and called me by his grace."

"How is it then, brethren? When ye comes together, everyone of you hath a psalm, hath an interpretation, let all things be done unto edifying. If any man speak in an unknown tongue, let it be by two or at the most by three and that by course; and let him keep silence in church; and let him speak to himself, and to God. Let the prophets speak two or three, and let the other judge." (I Corinthians 14:26-29).

This is a very good example of purpose. It shows each one has a purpose or a role to play. The gift shows the purpose. It does represent the purpose. It is also part of the purpose in one's life.

The purpose of the gift to sing is to give a psalm about God. The purpose of the gift to teach or preach the Word of God is to reveal God. It is to give people the doctrine or word of Christ who came to fulfill what God promised. The purpose of the gift of diverse tongues is to give different tongues in different languages. So is the gift of revelation to reveal what is hidden. The gift of interpretation is to interpret, and the gift of prophecy is to prophesy or to bring a message from the Holy Spirit to the church. All that shows the role a gift plays. It is there for a purpose.

We cannot have the same type of calling all of us. Some people are called to a local place; some to a nation; some to nations. We cannot all have the same anointing for service at the same time. But there is a particular(same) anointing transferred from person to person. Though the anointing may appear to be the same, for example, Elijah's anointing on Elisha, Moses' anointing on Joshua etc. Purposes are different and we flow according to the plan of the giver just like the scripture above has already guided us.

Check your purpose in line with your gift or grace. Flow in the spirit to prove and show the purpose and maturity in it. Don't wait for the purpose to mature in you. You should be the one to mature in the purpose for which you came for here on earth. Spiritual gifts don't mature. They are not like talents for them to mature. They are spiritual. It is you who matures in the spiritual gifts. Spiritual gifts are what they are and they don't change or mature like fruit. You just increase in levels as the anointing or power on you increases in line with the gift or calling upon your life. Ask for more anointing or infilling power of the Spirit. Otherwise, you already have the grace in your gifts. Those fivefold ministry gifts are graces. They are the anointing one was born with before you were formed in your mother's womb according to Jeremiah 1:5. Ordinations by your superiors are just an introduction of a person's ministry to the public because God anointed you before you were even formed. Ordination is an official launch into ministry.

You can see that Jesus Christ was officially ordained or announced by John the Baptist through baptism though John wanted Jesus to be the one to baptize him. John said he could not even carry the sandals (shoes) of Jesus Christ, but Jesus told John to go ahead and baptize Him for the sake of the fulfillment of the scriptures. And it was not that Jesus didn't know He was the one who was supposed to ordain and Baptize John the Baptist. Follow God's purpose or pattern, otherwise, you may end up depending on maturity instead of the anointing and the anointer.

So this is a powerful grouping of children of God which shows various purposes and gifting and callings. Each one is expected to produce what they have; to show what is contained in them. Each one must show their ability. Each one must show what they are good at, with talents to show and spiritual gifts to manifest. All this teaches us the purposes of individuals.

Let everyone in the church come with something. The Bible is clear on this.

This works well in small groupings or church or congregation. Whatever God gives you for the public, give it to the public. **Kenneth E Hagin** in one of his books said, "Pastors, get God's plan. Get down on your knees and stay there until you find out what His purpose is for your life and ministry."

One thing we must always be concerned about and ask ourselves is that, is it His purpose or mine? It is extremely sad and painful to flow and waste time in your purpose and not the purpose of God. God is not going to be in it if what you are doing is your manufactured purpose. Those expenses will not be met by God. You have to spend it by yourself. You have to bear your own mistakes or else cry for help if He has to come in. You have to find your own means to recover or spend. So don't take risks in plans God has not approved. He will not support them no matter how beautiful or sweet they are. There is no grace to them. You have to struggle to achieve. Make sure you have the right purpose with the right motive.

Don't imitate another person's individual purpose or gift or ministry or anointing or grace throughout your life. You have your own life purpose to fulfill. Unless you have nothing in that line, then you can serve under someone's grace and let them lay hands on you for you to have impartation anointing. Let imitation have limits. There is time for everything because the focus is Christ as Paul guided people at some point. Paul said imitate me as I imitate Christ. It will amount to laziness and envy if everything is imitated all the time. Copying another person's deeds all the time is not good for you. There is time to grow and mature in life and be responsible. You cannot be a child forever.

Fight hard to know your own grace and to flow in your own calling. Your life will show and prove to you if you are in the right place, the right plan and with the right people. Peace is a key, ***"pursue holiness and peace without which no man shall see the Lord,*** "the Bible says. Peace in your heart will be your compass to help you locate your grace. If you are lost, the same will help you locate where you missed. Listen to the heart. Listening to the heart is listening to the human spirit who is called the inner man or the inward man. Have the inward witness or the inward premonition directly connected to the Holy Ghost in you if you are regenerated or born again. Unless you are born again you cannot know all these things or God's will because you are driven by the Devil and the kingdom of darkness. Leave that side and be on the other side with God to fulfill the purpose and call God put on your life. Do it without delay to avoid God coming to question and say I never knew you, depart from me you wicked person.

God loves you and now is the time or never. God's work starts when you are born again, before that it is not His work. Instead it is just your work, and you will not be saved by works, but the scripture does not agree with that. You can understand His will in His Word when you are born again. Otherwise, without that, it is very difficult to sense God and His will upon your life because another god would be reigning in your heart. Romans 8:5-9; go up to verse-17 if you want for the complete context. So, you can't call God your Father if you are not born-again, and neither can He call you His child. It is only the children of God who have been given the gift of eternal life to live in the new paradise, who can call Him 'Father' and not those who have not accepted Christ as their Lord and personal Savior. One needs to accept Jesus Christ to come into their heart and regenerate them to be born again or become a new creation and reign in their hearts.

If you are not BORN AGAIN, you are of the kingdom of darkness and you can only call the Devil as your father, not God because He will come to say I never knew you, depart from me you wicked and you will be thrown in the lake of fire which burns with fire and brimstone. Now is the time for you to be born again. At the end of this book, you will see a prayer for salvation. Accept Jesus Christ to come into your heart and He will save you and reign in you. You will become born again, regenerated after that prayer. The Spirit of God, the Holy Spirit will bear witness that you are a child of God. You will know it and not doubt it as you continue to read the scriptures. Read especially the four gospels of Christ or the entire New Testament scriptures which are just a fulfillment of what was spoken in the Old Testament.

Chapter

- **6** -

FIND YOUR VISION

Habakkuk 2:1-3

"I will stand upon my watch, and set me upon the tower, and will watch to see what he will say unto me, and what I shall answer when I am reproved. And the LORD answered me, and said, write the vision, and make it plain upon tables, that he may run that readeth it. For the vision is yet for an appointed time, but at the end it shall speak, and not lie: though it tarry, wait for it; because it will surely come, it will not tarry"

A vision must be understood in a deeper way through the Spirit of God. The Holy Ghost gives the wisdom of interpretation.

Vision is seeing ahead as visualizing. Seeing words in pictures or images and you speak them into existence. Turning the words to substance. The vision becomes substance. Images of the mind become substance. Vision is foreknowledge of what is expected to happen before it takes place. You see it, feel it and have it.

You can never understand your purpose here on earth without a vision. Vision is a motivation. It must be a catalyst to motivate you until fulfillment. What you see or imagine as your vision to achieve in life must always motivate you to action, and if it motivates you then it must motivate your purpose, but know that it is not automatic. It may be a miss vision, not in line with your purpose as God's design, plan or discourse written or unwritten for your life. Purpose in life goes with motivation, zeal and vision. If you don't see it. If you don't visualize it. If you don't see your purpose, then there is no vision backing the purpose. Vision without purpose is not vision at all, but just a dream or ambition.

"Where there is no vision, the people perish..." (Proverbs 29:18).

See your purpose, let it be pictured, that is vision. If there is no vision of God backing the purpose, then the purpose is not from God and if there is no hint of God's purpose in the vision then the vision is not from God.

I John 5:4 **"for whatsoever is born of God overcometh the world: and this is the victory that overcometh the world, even our faith."**

What comes from God never fails, it has His backing. For as long as the purpose is from God it will come with a vision. And in a vision lies a plan. A vision without a plan from God in it to explain the purpose is not from God. The vision of God comes from heaven above while ambition comes from the earth. With that it is clear that if God is not in it, then it is an ambition which is wishful thinking, and it is earthly. No one gives himself a vision of God. If you give yourself a vision of God without His word or backing, then it is no longer a vision, but an ambition or career. A vision of God is God-made. An ambition is man-made. Ambition is earthly and not divine.

David Oyedepo said *"ambition is to do it better than others, it has a competitor, but vision has no competitor. If you have a competitor in your ministry or outside the ministry then what you are running is not* *a vision, but an ambition-fleshly thought or plan."*

Like it has earlier been said in Romans 11:29 *"for the gifts and calling of God are without repentance."*

Never use vision to compete. Instead do ministry by fulfilling the vision or do vision by fulfilling the ministry.

Philippians 3:14 *"I press toward the mark for the prize of the high calling of God in Christ Jesus"*

We need to work very hard without which there will be no ministry or purpose fulfillment.

A person can't have full understanding of vision until words become substance. Speak the vision in picture or image form of the mind until fulfillment of it. Fulfillment means reality.

Be prepared with the vision. You must be spiritually cooked for the public. Where there is no vision, people perish. God's vision has His backing and there is no struggle when He is involved. The vision born from God removes struggle on the way. You cannot limit the vision of God to the pulpit. It is not limited to the pulpit. The vision of God is beyond the pulpit. It is the unfolding of a divine plan for your life. Without it, people perish. You may be thinking what you have is a vision, yet it is an ambition-just your plan and people will perish as a result of that. Go back and listen properly. The most important thing is not to get a vision from yourself (ambition-man made), but from God.

May the Lord bless His vision and anointing upon you and destiny shall be sure. The world will hear about you whether hell likes it or not. Keep on going, run the vision. Let others who have seen the vision run it with you. It shall not tarry, but in due time it shall come to pass.

Romans 4:20 *"He **staggered not at the promise of God through unbelief; but was strong in faith, giving glory to God"***

FIND THE RIGHT PLAN

Proverbs 16:3

"commit thy works unto the LORD, and thy thoughts shall be established"

Proverbs 3:5-6

"Trust in the LORD with all thine heart; and lean not unto thine own understanding. In all thy ways acknowledge him, and he shall direct thy paths"

Proverbs 20:24

"Man's goings are of the LORD; how can a man then understand his own way?"

Proverbs 20:27

"The spirit of man is the candle of the LORD, searching all the inward parts of the belly"

God's plan or your plan? Your plans may not be God's plans. Your plans may not be God's purpose for your life. God's plans for your life will always be in line with your purpose for living.

Jeremiah 29:11 *"for I know the thoughts that I think toward you, saith the LORD, thoughts of peace, and not of evil, to give you an expected end"*

Isaiah 55:8 *"for my thoughts are not your thoughts, neither are your ways my ways, saith the LORD"*

Joshua 6:3-5

"And ye shall compass the city, all ye men of war, and go round about the city once. Thus shalt thou do six days. And seven priests shall bear before the ark seven trumpets of rams' horns: and the seventh day ye shall compass the city seven times, and the priests shall blow with the trumpets. And it shall come to pass, that when they make a long blast with the ram's horn, and when ye hear the sound of the trumpet, all the people shall shout with a great shout; and the wall of the city shall fall down flat, and the people shall ascend up every man straight before him"

II Kings 5:10

"And Elisha sent a messenger unto him, saying, Go and wash in Jordan seven times, and thy flesh shall come again to thee, and thou shalt be clean"

Ephesians 2:10

"For we are his workmanship, created in Christ Jesus unto good works, which God hath before ordained that we should walk in them. Let your plans be in line with the plans of God. Follow the plans of God, they make a way, they pave the way and if the way is paved it means it is smooth; it means grace, and grace is unmerited favor; favor with no labor, favor without working for it. Favor without sweat"

There is always a time for sweet and a time for sweat. There is always a season for that. You can only find sweet in the line of calling and talent. God likes it when you begin to flow in the calling He gave you because that is what He wants. That is His will. He hates it when you go off track because there is no grace in the off track. There is no protection there. There is no involvement of God. There is no blessing of God. It means you are walking alone. He cannot support what He did not start. God does support what He did not initiate. That is the way God is. His thoughts are not like man's thoughts, by far.

Isaiah 55:11 ***"So shall my word be that goeth forth out of my mouth: it shall not return unto me void, but it shall accomplish that which I please, and it shall prosper in the thing whereto I sent it"***

FIND THE RIGHT PLACE

No matter how powerful you are, if the place where you are being not right, it will finish you including everything you have. That place is meant for another person's anointing. The one God designated for that place should be there, not your anointing. You cannot operate your anointing in every place. You will end up blunting it and fail if you force things. Sense if you were not meant to be where you are.

Where your friend is running away from, maybe is where your anointing fits. Where you failed, maybe is where your friend's anointing was meant to succeed. You need to sense that. The anointing doesn't have a problem. What matters is the right place. Have you found the right place? Because in the right place EVERYTHING FLOWS. In the wrong place LITTLE OR NOTHING FLOWS. Instead you begin to go down. Everything begins to fall apart. God did bless Adam and Eve with the right place, at the right time in the Garden of Eden.

Genesis 2:8-15

"and the LORD God planted a garden eastward in Eden; and there he put the man whom he had formed. And out of the ground made the LORD God to grow every

tree that is pleasant to the sight, and good for food...And a river went out of Eden to water the garden; and from thence it was parted, and became into four heads.

The name of the first is Pison: that is, it which compasseth the whole land of Havilah, where there is gold; and the gold of that land is good: there is bdellium and the onyx stone. And the name of the second river is Gihon: the same is it that compasseth the whole land of Ethiopia. And the name of the third river is Hiddekel: that is it which goeth toward the east of Assyria. And the fourth river is Euphrates. And the LORD God took the man, and put him into the Garden of Eden to dress it and to keep it."

Act 17:26

"and hath made...all nations of men for to dwell on all the face of the earth, and hath determined...the bounds of their habitation"

The Garden of Eden was the right place, and it was God's choice, born of God and sealed by God to cover a person in everything and to provide every need.

It is important to know the right place to operate in where there is grace. Please find that place with the right people and the right plan backed by God Almighty.

When God created Adam, He first made a place for him. Before you were formed in your mother's womb God had already planned your life.

The earth was big, but not every place was good for Adam. He could have liked to be in any other place if he had a personal choice, but life could have been bad and difficult for him in another place other than the Garden of Eden which had everything and was well-watered. God's plan and choice in this case is the best.

God made sure Adam was located in a particular place. The question is, have you located in the right place, or have you become a vagabond or nomadic in your movements in trying to settle? That would mean there is no vision yet. Every vision has a location. Every ministry has a location to find you and where everything is born or starts from.

A God-chosen place is an anointed place. A God chosen place is the place of grace. A place chosen by you is not. It may actually be a place of struggle without proper wisdom about it. If you want to struggle, move by your thoughts. That is why the Bible says, *"...lean not unto thine own*

understanding' 'thoughts Proverbs 3:5. It says, ***"...in all your ways acknowledge him and he shall direct your path."***

That is the way to locate Him. That is the way to locate His plan. That is the way to locate the right people He has chosen to work with you. It is not every place. It is not every plan. It is not every person, but certain people. It is not every place, but certain place. It is not every plan, but a certain plan. All those must be divine.

Adam was placed in the Garden of Eden. The exact place God had chosen, prepared, and planned for him. The grace in Eden was that it had everything in it. It had four rivers surrounding it to water it consistently. God's blessings will only meet you when you are in the right place. Until you locate your place you will continue to struggle with your wisdom and succeed in your wisdom. That is the battle, and it is the greatest battle of your life. But the place first, then the plan, then the right people. Don't be fond of moving from one place to another without God in it, you will ruin your ministry.

Don't envy others and their successes if you have started your own journey of fulfilling your vision. You will lose yours in the process. You will end up fulfilling other people's dreams. Don't waste all your lifetime in fulfilling other people's individual visions if you were meant to fulfill yours too. You may use those employers to get there, but many people have spent years and years working for others who have prospered using them and have gained nothing. It is good for the employers with their employees especially if the employee has no vision of self-independence. It is not bad if you are getting paid as an employee. If you are called to your own, start thinking and planning to employ. There are those who are lost in their real plan.

It is good to first work for another. Some people have not yet found their place and the right people to fulfill their personal lives. Use them as employees and build them to realize their potential. Many people first work for somebody before they realize their potential and there is nothing wrong with that. If the employer is the right person the employee has found, work with him or her as an employer. It is the same vice versa. If your place is the right place for them and they fit into your plans or vision by divine arrangement, let them work with you. Maybe they have arrived in a place God meant for them and make sure that place is producing results, full of grace. Don't fail to pay them.

Many people have comfortably spent years fulfilling other people's visions, putting theirs aside or completely abandoning theirs which they were born for. Unless they are learning from them or they were divinely meant to work or sit under someone's anointing, they were wasting their time.

Don't waste time while you are working on another person's plan. Start to invest well to build your own, but don't create a vision within a vision. What will you say before God if He asked you what you did with what He gave you on earth? With the purpose He gave you? With the gifts, the anointing, and the calling He gave you? Fulfill the purpose why you came here on earth.

There is no place like the place ordained by God. It has all the support by God to defend it and to attack any negativity or enemy attacking it. If you have found the right vision, anointing, gift, grace, you will be surrounded by divine protection in order to fulfill. All born of God overcomes the world. The place will speak. In case you are still lost. In case you still doubt where you are. The place will speak volumes if you are in the right place.

Keep going by the Spirit of God through divine revelation, not your head. Get revelation from God, not from your head. Let the heart help you, not the mind. That heart should be full of the Word of God because God cannot speak to you without using His word. You have to meditate on the Word of God. The Word of God is a lamp; it is a light to your path. Without it you may not see where you are going. You may be moving in darkness. Without it is like walking with a gun without bullets. When you bring in the Word you simply bring in the light. Without the light (Word) you cannot see and know what is in your house (in your heart). Nobody likes to walk in the dark without the light. So, the Word of God is light.

You shouldn't like to move anywhere or stay anywhere without the revelation of God to guide. The place may be tough for you.

Abraham was told to go to a land or country he never knew and found the place approved by God. When God approves the place, He has already given the light. You just need to stay there. If God has not spoken or approved the place, don't make it a permanent place. You just have to leave the place. It may be fit for another and not you. Let God approve your vision in line with His will.

FINDTHE RIGHT PEOPLE

Proverbs 18:24

*"A **man that hath friends must shew himself friendly: and there is a friend that sticketh closer than a brother"***

Proverbs 20:6

"Most men will proclaim every one his own goodness: but a faithful man who can find?"

The right people are not people that give you money; that feed you; that sit by your bedside when you are sick or when down. Even your enemies can do that. You can be given money by your enemy, you can be fed by your enemy, you can be dressed by your enemy, and you can be visited by your enemy on a bedside where you are sick or down.

Don't be excited that the people who do such things are right the people. The only right people are the people God has chosen. God's chosen people to live in your life as destiny helpers. God's chosen people to live in your life are those who accompany. Very few of the ones God has chosen walk out of your life unless they were just meant to escort you a certain mile, but they still stay in faith that you will succeed and they don't forget you. They come back and comfort or support you when you are in problems. God's right chosen people to live in your life accompany, but enemies of the wrong or right people don't last long, they are temporal and so shall they be in your life. So, they are right now. There are two types of enemies.

Those you call **wrong people** and those you call **right people**, but both are not your friends, but enemies. Wrong people-enemies and right people-enemies. Let us look at them.

The ones you perceive or call **wrong people**, they are mostly enemies who don't pretend because you see their wrongs. But the ones you call or perceive to be the **right people** in your own thinking because they are doing right to you and what you expected, are mostly enemies and they pretend. They are the ones who pretend. You won't see their wrong; you will see their wrong later. You must always wait; always have patience and study every situation, good or bad to you. These are the most dangerous people. It is said that the enemy you know is better than the enemy you don't know.

The enemy you don't know works with traps. Those you know, they know you know. They show their works, and you face them squarely in response. You manage to fight back, but those you don't know who work with traps are difficult to fight. Satan is one of them apart from people. Satan traps because you don't see him and you don't know him. He may do very good things to you, buy vehicles for you, buy sweets, soft drinks, cake, ice cream etc. But, you may not know it was a trap. He did that to Adam and Eve. What about you and me today? He tried to do that to Jesus Christ during 40 days fasting; what about you and me today? When the Bible says, **"who can find a virtuous woman?"** does not just show you how expensive it is, but also shows a trap that can be involved by the enemy planting the wrong seed as you go in search for such a woman. That is why it is a question. In the Garden of Eden, the enemy said you shall not surely die. There was a trap using the words of God. Always be careful with traps. They come through what is already good and you may not see any wrong unless the Spirit of God reveals the trap involved.

There will be people who will pretend until you fall into their trap and think it is God who has given you. **"A perfect gift comes from above..."** God's choice is the best. It may look bad in your eyes. If God is in it, get it. He will perfect it to the fullest for the happiness of the rest of your life and you will not tire of testifying His goodness. That is how the perfect will of God is. Permissive will is where you have made a wrong choice, but the thing chosen is looking good, man-made choice.

Romans 8:4

"That the righteousness of the law might be fulfilled in us, who walk not after the flesh, but after the Spirit"

There are two types of friends there on that scripture above, choose which friend you will work with or walk with.

Proverbs 27:6

Faithful *are* the wounds of a friend; but the kisses of an enemy *are* deceitful

Chapter

-7-

A JOURNEY OF FAITH

Genesis 5:24

"And Enoch walked with God: and he was not; for God took him"

Hebrews 11:5

"By faith Enoch was translated that he should not see death; and was not found, because God had translated him: for before his translation he had this testimony, that he pleased God"

A journey of faith is a walk of action. It is not a walk in fear which is a negative weapon. A faith walk is a walk to obtain a good report like the elders did obtain according to (Hebrews 11:2).

Faith in action is faith by acting on God's word. It is not just a mouth faith without acting on what you say or imagine. It is doing what the word of God says and it is not about choosing smooth things and simple things for yourself or anybody.

What is very tough, torturing and time-wasting is your own thoughts, places, plans which are not backed by God; where God is not in, and you have no grace? There is no reward for such. God is not a fool to reward what He did not sanction. For as long as God has not sanctioned what you are doing, you are bleeding for nothing and sweating for nothing. Let God help you so that you don't go very far in the wrong direction because some things are difficult to end or to come out from them when they start. It is difficult to throw in the towel or wash your hands in a situation where you are used to and affects other people. Especially if people look at you as a role model. You need to take your time or else you will crush others in the process. You may cause others to fall or backslide and stop following God.

A journey of faith in something you are sacrificing your full life for should be sanctioned by God. The God-given vision, place, people etc., is the true journey of faith to sacrifice for. Outside that you are sailing on a destiny of fruitless journey.

Spending years walking in faith requires action by investing all you can in the will of God. God's gift should be the first to invest in with whatever resources you have. Faith is not just waiting. Faith is using what you have rightly in His will according to the grace you have.

"But without faith it is impossible to please him; for he that cometh to God must believe that he is, and that he is a rewarder of them that diligently seek him. (Hebrews 11:6).

God is a rewarder-HE IS A REWARDER-of those who DILIGENTLY (seriously)SEEK HIM.

Seek God in His word and do His word to see exploits. No matter how difficult the situation is in your life God will turn it for good for you who love Him and are the called according to His purpose. If the word is approved by God, you will not go down. Shame may be for a short period.

"The Lord is the Strength of my life; of whom shall I be afraid." (Psalm 27:1).

Faith in God should be faith in His word because faith in His Word is faith in God. If you and I have faith in God, then we have faith in His Word. You can't have faith in God, but you don't have faith in His Word. You can't have faith in His Word, but you don't have faith in God, then something is terribly wrong with your life.

MY WALK IN FAITH

Walking in faith is walking in the Word. It is walking in Christ. Walk in Christ Jesus for everything as you act on what you believe in and what is in line with His Word.

I spent many years trying to discover myself. I walked as an evangelist throughout the years and stuck to it. I didn't know that it was not a major office for me, just a supplement to the major call. Most of the things I produced were more than one grace of an evangelist. It was apostolic anointing. People who saw that spoke about it to confirm. God could communicate with me through His Word and showed me the difference. God taught me that it was not the title that determined who you are, but it was the work. What you bring out will determine the title. That is what speaks volumes. It speaks volumes to people who see the difference.

Friends and many other people began to get concerned with my calling as an evangelist. They told me they see more works than just of an evangelist. "We only see little of an evangelist in you," but I was popular as an evangelist countrywide and beyond. "We see many ministries in you as in the five-fold ministry. Of all those five offices, the evangelist ministry is leading after apostolic ministry."

Well vested people did confirm that I was an apostle. I was in the works of an apostle. I faced a greater challenge and resistance over my calling from a friend when I was preaching in a foreign land of Zimbabwe. When I ministered to people that got wind about how God uses me. When I got into Botswana by faith with little money and came back with victory to the surprise of everyone. From a very little money I had used; going to a place to meet a person I have never met in my life. And it was for the first time, all related to the calling of an apostle in their view.

The word I ministered in one of the meetings organized in Zimbabwe, which brought different churches together, even I couldn't understand the greatness that was in it. While I was preaching, the whole crowd went begging and shouting. They were begging me to buffer the Word because it was too much for them to handle. What really happened was that some people underrated me by seeing me physically and it couldn't tally with what they expected. So that pierced my spirit, aroused my boldness, and stirred up my anointing.

And I ministered prophetically strengthened by the Spirit of God.

When I ministered the Word of God and stopped by the leading of the Holy Ghost, during preaching people had gotten tired of begging me to spare them with the message for it was too powerful. I decided to sit down for a while with a certain evangelist(friend) who wanted to speak into my life. He first decided to check my Bible and found a lot of shaded portions of Scriptures. To him, that was enough confirmation of my calling. He told me I was not an evangelist, but an Apostle. He said I was wasting time with the title of evangelist. He presented a lot of arguments to me and stated that he doesn't miss when he makes such analysis. He had many men of God he spoke to similarly. I told him to just pause the argument and know that I would not change my title even if I was an Apostle inside. He left me with words that I would come back to him to confirm, because he doesn't easily miss. He left me in deep thoughts, and I took it to God.

Today I want to go back to him in Zimbabwe to confirm that he was right. He was helping me. It was true in my spirit, and I feel I wasted a lot of time operating in areas I had little grace. Whatever you flow in by force, which God has not ordained, it will be the permissive will of God. I only survived the argument because the gift of an evangelist also works for me greater than other offices in the fivefold ministry apart from the office of an apostle.

My heart pours towards evangelistic missions and it is very comfortable in massive evangelistic movements other than other things or just person to person evangelism. Though my major office can be apostle, which makes me flow in all other four ministries, the most effective ministry I flow in is the ministry of an evangelist, unless otherwise. The office of an apostle and the office of an evangelist have similarities. They are both itinerant in nature. The office of an evangelist in me branches out from apostolic base. What it means is that the office of an apostle has all those four offices in it. He can operate in the office of a pastor, evangelist, prophet, and teacher. He can pastor. He can evangelize. He can prophesy. He can teach. An apostle can flow in all those four as a full grace of the call of an apostle. He has limited grace on each of those gifts depending on the situation as the Spirit of God leads him in a particular gift each time. If you have full grace in one of those four gifts, then you are not an apostle and you should not call yourself that. It is believed that an apostle flows in all the four, not just one. Not one grace, but four graces in one person.

I was tutored in spiritual matters by Kenneth E. Hagin directly for about 10 years before he died. Through him I learned to flow in the power gifts such as the gift of healings, the gift of workings of miracles and the gift of faith. I learned how to be led by the Spirit of God. I learned praying by quoting Scriptures in faith and positive confession. I learned discerning of spirits, and partly the word of wisdom. I tested all other nine gifts of the Holy Ghost before. It definitely produced greater results. I mainly flew in power gifts and revelation gifts, but less in inspirational or utterance gifts. I also learned about revelation gifts partly from Richard Roberts, the son of Oral Roberts. I learnt from him too the gift of word of knowledge. Due to this I sometimes preach prophetically when in a huge audience. I even see people's problems and futures. I don't begin to prophesy to individuals but preach to them all and they begin to cry. Each one feels they are being spoken to directly, especially the ones the Word is spiritually targeting. I spend time looking at that person if I am directed when I am preaching, and various manifestations begin to take place.

My spiritual father, Apostle Frank Mutale, based in South Africa, played a big part in my life. I will never ever forget. What a great man of God that he is. He taught me spiritual warfare and Word-based prayer. He introduced me to Charles Grandson Finney materials at an early stage. I followed Smith Wigglesworth by the leading of the Spirit. I followed Benny Hinn, Reinhard Bonnke, T. D. Jakes, and Billy Graham. Graham strongly made me know how to begin a ministry not necessarily a church. I strongly followed Morris Cerullo introduced to me by some men of God who were following my spiritual father's steps. Because of Morris Cerullo being moved by Charles G. Finney's ministry, who I was earlier connected to via materials by my spiritual father, it gave me indirect connection to Charles Finney through tapping from

Morris Cerullo. Morris Cerullo used to cry in his preaching each time he testified about Charles Finney. I wanted to know how Morris was flowing by following Charles G. Finney.

Some great men of God I have mentioned impacted me a lot. Some impacted my life through listening to their audios and not reading their books. Some it was reading their books, but not listening to their audios. It is funny, but just follow the leading of the Spirit, through your spirit. Follow what He wants you to feed on and how and from whom? I followed other great men of God like John G. Lake, John Knox etc. I will write about them in other books.

Half of my Christian life was too much driven by Kenneth E. Hagin who taught and mentored me for about 10 years every month before he died. I followed his pattern on the Spirit of God, the Word of God and faith not overlooking declarations. I learnt to quote the word of God.

And my spiritual father shook the foundations of my spiritual life to a solid one based on the word and the spirit that produced greater miracles I have ever known and seen to date. I saw Reinhard Bonnke in my dream vision. The Spirit of God telling me in a dream the type of anointing which was upon him that it was on me too. I wrote to Bonnke about the dream I had about him having what was on me. He couldn't believe it. I kept it to my heart and left it to God since I didn't create the dream. I will testify of how mighty I have moved in power or miracles in other books to come that are fully going to talk about the ministry of the Holy Ghost.

I have a book I am still editing which I have entitled THE HOLY SPIRIT TODAY-VOLUME 1 where I am addressing the miracles I have witnessed in my life and in those men and women of God we know. I want to address them one by one to also analyze their strengths and secrets to greater miracles they experienced in their lives. This book **'Discovering God's Purpose for your Life'** goal is for the reader to discern the will and purpose of God for his or her life. Someone in a different country has also written about my life walking in the power of the Spirit of God, which is a great thing. And I appreciate this good friend of mine, Pastor Jacob. Better someone talks about you than you talk about yourself. It carries more weight and gives a good appeal to the public. Just like people such as Dr. Luke who wrote about the apostle Paul and not himself.

I equally experienced greater miracles from a very young stage. God was proving Himself to me. He began to introduce Himself to me in greater and untold miracles like those we see in the Bible. By His grace I will come to testify when I am teaching on the gifts of the Holy Ghost and the Holy Ghost Himself as a person as I earlier stated above.

So just here not to go too far on knowing your grace, I spent three-quarters of my life in a miss of my real calling. I followed Bro. Hagin until he died to learn how he arrived at his final calling and ministry and finish in it to the last breath of his life. He pastored many churches until he pastored his own and led his ministry. He confirmed that he was not in the perfect will of God, and he flew by limited grace until in his main calling or grace. Many have learned from him especially me by closely following him from a distance; unlike others who lived in the United States of America.

What makes me happy now is that finally my spiritual father also confirmed my calling as an apostle over the calling of an evangelist, after spending years of arguing and flowing in an office which showed little fruit. By that, I mean I was sticking to just one ministry unconfirmed instead of sticking first to the leadership of the Holy Ghost. He is the one in charge of the body of Christ until this world comes to an end. He directly affects your life, my life. Thank God for His leadership. We must get back to our spiritual calling and gifts. There are people who can speak into your life. Please have them too. It is better for your life other than moving headless. Now it is confirmed that I am an apostle to the body of Christ and an evangelist to the world. (The apostle, Paul, admonished Pastor Timothy to do the work of an evangelist, II Timothy 4:5.)

I had to travel to South Africa for confirmation of my calling when many, many people had already confirmed. So, the final confirmation about my calling was my spiritual father. He saw this when I was one month in Christ, but performing miracles. He gave the exact word people have been saying, that you are not just an evangelist, but an apostle. As if he was there where many people kept confirming from man of God to another. And he prayed for me and finally released me into ministry, though I was ordained in 1998 by Evangelistic Messengers Association International-USA (EMA) which started in 1933.EMA even sent me the ordination certificate and license to preach worldwide, but I was ordained publicly as an apostle in Zimbabwe in 2018. This happened by my good and great friend before a big number of witnesses in his church called Upper Room Ministries.

My friend, apostle Mudimba, accepted the revelation of public ordination in my life, which many people confirmed everywhere even before I was finally ordained in the office of an apostle. Today I feel safe and at peace. I feel like I have just begun. Like Paul and Barnabas were separated and repositioned into their real grace, which is the lesson example which we are learning in this book. All this confirmed in my spirit that I was an apostle: I am an apostle with an evangelist ministry.

I have two great and public assignments:

1. To the **body of Christ** through the anointing of an apostle

2. To the **world** through the anointing of an evangelist

Both assignments have one mission: **to make disciples** (of Christ).

In the body of Christ my business is to **groom or train the saved or those born again**. In the world my business is to **bring the lost** into the body of Christ to be groomed by groomers. Thus, apostle and evangelist titles both vested in me and I feel strongly that I must be ordained in both, not just one as an apostle. That is my spiritual sensation at the moment. And, soon I will seek to also be ordained as an evangelist, if my God permits. I know He will because I always sense it in my spirit like ordination is not complete. I have finally I attained a level of studies as Doctor of Practical Theology and sailing in various studies like biblical studies, religious studies, computer studies and thank God for my mentors the late Dr. David J. Ford, who has been President of EMA and my tutor and mentor Dr. J. R. Keller, both of the USA. God bless the team and those leading currently. Dr. Keller has been there for me.

Finally, the last chapter of the book shows two needs as the will of God: land and farming for Abraham, Isaac, and Jacob to prosper. The Abrahamic covenant of prosperity didn't leave them with nothing to do.

133

Chapter

-8 -

FARMING THE WILL OF GOD

Genesis 2:8-15

"and the LORD God planted a garden eastward in Eden; and there he put the man whom he had formed. And out of the ground made the LORD God to grow every tree that is pleasant to the sight, and good for food...And a river went out of Eden to water the garden; and from thence it was parted, and became into four heads.

The name of the first is Pison: that is it which compasseth the whole land of Havilah, where there is gold; And the gold of that land is good: there is bdellium and the onyx stone. And the name of the second river is Gihon: the same is it that compasseth the whole land of Ethiopia. And the name of the third river is Hiddekel: that is it which goeth toward the east of Assyria. And the fourth river is Euphrates. And the LORD God took the man, and put him into the Garden of Eden to dress it and to keep it."

Genesis 3:17-19

"And unto Adam he said, Because thou hast hearkened unto the voice of thy wife, and hast eaten of

*the tree, of which I commanded thee,
saying, Thou shalt not eat of it: cursed is
the ground for thy sake; in sorrow shalt
thou eat of it all the days of thy
life; Thorns also and thistles shall it bring
forth to thee; and thou shalt eat the herb
of the field; In the sweat of thy face shalt
thou eat bread, till thou return unto the
ground; for out of it wast thou taken: for
dust thou art, and unto dust shalt thou
return."*

Genesis 3:23-24

*"Therefore **the LORD God sent him forth
from the Garden of Eden, to till the
ground from whence he was taken. So
he drove out the man; and he placed at
the east of the garden of Eden
Cherubims, and a flaming sword which
turned every way, to keep the way of the
tree of life."***

Farming is the will of God. It was the first job God gave to man. And this job is general and a call to all to go into it given the chance. There is no trace of poverty in farming, especially if you center on cash crops and animal husbandry. Almost all Bible men of God prospered from it. God is called God of Abraham, Isaac, and Jacob. They were all farmers and animal husbandmen; and prospered from it to the point of great financial wealth. But the interest here is land. What shall you do with land? Minerals are also in the ground. From soil is where all riches are. All animals go down to the soil. I have not known one that does not. If there is, it will be very interesting. So, we must teach prosperity first from land, the soil. There are hidden treasures in the soil. (Speak to the earth by the word of the Lord and command those treasures be released to you. Isaiah 1:2; Jeremiah 22:29; Revelation 12:16))

As a man of God or child of God or as a person, know that farming is the will of God. And the best that describes what God said: **"I will bless the works of your hands."**

The riches of Abraham, Isaac, and Jacob and many other great men and women of God in the Bible came from farming the land, not from minerals, not mining, but farming. Minerals, Jesus has also talked about them. They are also hidden treasures in the ground, but I want you to view smart farming as clean business and more lucrative.

And farming is not just planting or growing anything you think in your head for as long as it will grow. You must be a smart farmer as a person, as a man of God or a child of God or woman of God. Smart farming is picking cash crops. And specific things that can easily make you great and generate cash flow in the shortest possible time without depending solely on the seasonal rains. It is also important to harness the water coming from the ground. Water on the ground is there. Three-fourths of the earth is covered by water to cleanse the ground and feed the sky by evaporation to recycle it. It is a system God has made. God controls this system. Man can also control it in the way that he wants it. Thus far we have advanced in this world to control weather temporarily. Man can even decide where the rains can fall if he doesn't want it in his area. I have tackled these issues in my other book yet to be out which is entitled THE SECOND COMING OF CHRIST.

Land is the number one blessing God wants you to have. It is not just for building a house or a structure of your desire, but to utilize it wisely. Farming on land meets almost every need you can find from a supermarket. I have had great knowledge to do great things in farming in the shortest period of time I have interacted with some people involved in farming. We were championing organic fertilizer and value crops.

Some things have come as God's revelation in the area of farming. I am showing you something to start with as you decide to reposition yourself. Position yourself in the right calling, place or purpose. Poverty is a choice.

As a man of God, as a child of God or just as a person, you cannot be poor following the route of farming. If you should not be directly involved, have direct knowledge to direct a manager of your farm. Concentrate to grow cash crops you want and run high value animals you want. This is what can make you as rich as people like Abraham, Isaac, Jacob etc., who had the anointing to do that. The question is, are you anointed to be blessed and be a blessing to others? The answer is yes! In Genesis when God created man and woman, he blessed them. He told them to be fruitful and to multiply. If you are born again, you are even in a better position because you are directly in the covenant of Abraham of prosperity and good health. So, if you are, then you are anointed to be blessed. In other words, you are blessed so rise up and act on it. If land has finished where you are, find it somewhere else. If you can't find it buy it from the one who has it. If you are not managing, then pray to God to give you another way of prospering. You can get the hidden treasures of darkness, they are yours. One of them is minerals but own a mine not looking for pieces to dupe people, own a mine. It is possible by all legal means.

Minerals are yours. I would not go for that myself though it is in the will of God as God-given. I would rather go Abraham's way and that is farming though he was also rich in minerals. Even Adam and Eve had the chance to mine minerals in the Garden of Eden. Instead, they ignored and went farming. You cannot eat minerals, buy or sell though at a point they can bring in greater sums of money. They are for other use-decoration and other products out of them. Farming is better and the best as a source of living or business. That is if you have finally found the line of your calling, grace, purpose of anointing. This far you have read this book, by now it should help you also know a better business you can do as you discover the Lord's purpose for your life. This book is for correction and guidance. It puts you straight to know who you are and what God has already done and revealed for you to do. Revisit your entire life.

Farming was the first ministry or job God gave to Adam or a human being. Farming, as a way of life, provides sustenance and eliminates poverty and the possibility of starving people. They shouldn't starve. God will never accept any apologies to that. As a man of God or Child of God or just a person created in the image of God, you must bring to an end the poverty and suffering of your family. Poverty of food, wearing and drinking (not of alcohol) should come to an end. These three areas of lack originate from farming or the lack thereof. Let us not depend on the rain all the time. We have enough water on the ground, use a drip irrigation system.

There is a water table from where we can have a constant flow of water to reach whatever we have planted. By choosing to farm we need to prosper because demand for food will always be there. When God called you, He didn't call your wife. He didn't call your children. Today the clergy use starvation as an excuse to fast. When you have failed to provide, don't declare a fast in your family just fast by yourself and let them eat. Don't starve people. Do you know that you can go to hell for that? Failing to provide does not mean failing to keep your wife and family. You can't starve your family forever and ever. God will not let you starve people you keep because God cannot starve you or your family. He provides every day and He is willing to provide even beyond what you think or expect. Pray for direction. Pray for the right friends in life. Pray for the right place of blessings and the right time of blessings. Reposition your grace. Reposition your anointing, your calling, and plan. Check the people you are found with if they add value and ask for forgiveness from God for missing His mark. He will help you reposition yourself to your grace. Whatever does not add value to your life or change you to the will of God, change it before it changes you and finishes you up. We must increase our trust and totally depend on Him. That is absolute dependence on God which is absolute faith in God.

Let me give you the mind of God by Jesus Christ for Scriptural backing of the will of God on using the ground first of all for farming and then minerals if you can. Jesus Christ used the two as an example in most of his teachings.

Matthew 13:1-9, 18-23 Farming land

Matthew 13: 24-30 Farming land

Matthew 13:31-32 Farming land

Matthew 13:33 Farming land

Matthew 13:44-46 Minerals-Mining land

Matthew 13:47-50 Fishing, another form of animal husbandry

Finally, let me take my time to lead you into accepting Jesus Christ as your Lord and personal Savior. You have read this book. Aim sure God has spoken to you in many ways. You have noticed your area's weakness and mistakes and you want to flow in His will. But, if you are a sinner, He cannot begin to use you in your exact life purpose and calling. You are the temple of the Devil. Accept Jesus Christ today and that is when your life purpose and program will begin to tick to the glory of God in His book of records. If you don't come back to your senses and repent, He will come to say, "I never knew you, depart from me, you sinner..." Will that be okay for you? If it will not be okay and if it is not okay now, then praying this prayer of salvation below:

A PRAYER OF SALVATION:

Say, 'heavenly Father, I have heard your word which has been spoken to me in this book. I realize that I am a sinner and lost. I lost direction. I have decided to come back to you my Creator. I ask you to forgive me of all sins I have ever done in my life. I ask you to cleanse me of all of them. Now, I ask Jesus Christ your Son who came in the flesh, who died for me on the cross of Calvary, to come into my heart and be my Lord and personal Savior. Regenerate my spirit to be put right with you and in tune with your Spirit. Lord, I ask you right now to delete my name from the Book of Death and write it in the Book of Life. Fill me with your Holy Spirit. I thank you in Jesus Christ's name, Amen! Thank you, heavenly Father, for saving my life. Thank you for making me born again today, Amen!'

If you have prayed that prayer above, you are now one of us. You are now part of the Kingdom of Christ, the Kingdom of God Almighty. You have been translated from the kingdom of darkness to the kingdom of light. You are no longer a member of the kingdom of darkness. Your name has been deleted from it, rejoice! Thousands of angels in heaven are now celebrating over your coming back to your Creator. So, no matter what, your name is written or entered in the book of life. Stand brave and help your friends and family the same way. Build yourself up on this Scripture, Colossians 2:6-10:

"as ye have therefore received Christ Jesus the Lord, sowalk ye in him: Rooted and built up in him, and stablished in the faith...abounding therein with thanksgiving. Beware lest any man spoil you through philosophy and vain deceit, after the tradition of men, after the rudiments of the world,

and not after Christ. For in him dwelleth all the fullness of the Godhead bodily. And ye are complete in him, which is the head of all principality and power."

Find a full gospel Bible believing church. Let them baptize you with the baptism pattern of Jesus Christ which was conducted by John the Baptist. Then be baptized with the Holy Spirit too as the scripture says. If you can't find a church to help you grow, let us know. We have to know how we can help you to grow and become a soul winner too. Contact us to help you.

To continue in spiritual tune with me and my team or if you wish to donate your material or financial support for the spread of the gospel through books and other media:

Contact: +260763988703 / +260950595611 / +260979011557

Email: chileshegregory@gmail.com

:doctorgregorypublications@gmail.com
:omegachampions2024@gmail.com
:omegaprintingandpublishing@gmail.com
Visit Web: drgregorychileshe.com

www.ingramcontent.com/pod-product-compliance
Lightning Source LLC
Chambersburg PA
CBHW071623150726
48000CB00004B/1860